AMERICA PLAYS BALL

Historical Baseball Photographs from the Library of Congress

A BOOK OF POSTCARDS

SAN FRANCISCO

Pomegranate Communications, Inc.
Box 808022, Petaluma CA 94975
800-227-1428
www.pomegranate.com

Pomegranate Europe Ltd.
Unit 1, Heathcote Business Centre, Hurlbutt Road
Warwick, Warwickshire CV34 6TD, UK
[+44] 0 1926 430111

ISBN 0-7649-3208-X
Pomegranate Catalog No. AA282

© 2005 Library of Congress

Pomegranate publishes books of
postcards on a wide range of subjects.
Please contact the publisher for more information.

Researched and compiled by Nicholas Osborne

Cover designed by Lora Santiago
Printed in China
14 13 12 11 10 09 08 07 06 05   10 9 8 7 6 5 4 3 2 1

To facilitate detachment of the postcards from this book, fold each card along its perforation line before tearing.

"I see great things in baseball," wrote Walt Whitman in 1846. "It's our game—the American game. It will take our people out-of-doors, fill them with oxygen, give them a larger physical stoicism. Tend to relieve us from being a nervous, dyspeptic set. Repair these losses, and be a blessing to us." But more than a century later, in 1985, Commissioner of Major League Baseball Bart Giamatti criticized what he saw as the commercialism inherent in the late-twentieth-century game: "In a fashion typically American, baseball carried a lore at variance with its behavior; it promoted its self-image as green game while it became a business. That gap in baseball between first promise and eventual execution is with us to this day."

Whitman's words about the powers of baseball may be naive, but neither does Giamatti's view that baseball was never a "green game" accurately convey the way many people first encounter it. The photographs collected in this volume, taken from the 1900s to the 1950s, illustrate arguably the largest role baseball has ever played in the United States: not as a commercial sport, but as a pastime enjoyed by people young and old, male and female, East and West.

America Plays Ball ranges from farms to coal mines, sandlot to slag pile, backyards to military bases to the grounds of the US Capitol. One of the earliest photographs shows quite formally dressed men and women playing to while away an afternoon. Elsewhere, older players attend an organized game in view of the Washington Monument, while young ones take a few impromptu swings beside a schoolhouse during recess. Baseball appears at important markers in American history: farm workers play in a field in Arkansas during the Great Depression; during World War II, GIs play ball, and so do Japanese Americans in the Manzanar internment camp. The fields in *America Plays Ball* range from well-groomed diamonds to Arctic glaciers, and teams formed from student bodies, local leagues, and political parties can be found.

These postcards demonstrate how people of many places and times have discovered the pleasure of baseball. Whitman also wrote that "the game of ball is glorious," a sentiment with which those pictured here would doubtless agree. *America Plays Ball* shows the diverse forms that glory can take. In every instance, it reminds the viewer of baseball's ability to bring simple joy to those who play it.

—Nicholas Osborne

AMERICA PLAYS BALL

Hitting the ball in Rock Creek Park, Washington DC, July 1942.
Photograph by John Ferrell
Prints and Photographs Division, LC-USF34-011599-D

CA 94975

PETALUMA

BOX 808022

Pomegranate

AMERICA PLAYS BALL

US Resettlement Administration project children's baseball game at
Granger (IA) Homesteads, May 1936.

Photograph by Carl Mydans

Prints and Photographs Division, LC-USF33-T01-607-M5

CA 94975

PETALUMA

BOX 808022

Pomegranate

AMERICA PLAYS BALL

Playground, Banneker Junior High School, Washington DC, March 1942.
Photograph by Marjory Collins

Prints and Photographs Division, LC-USW3-965-E

BOX 808022   PETALUMA   CA 94975

Pomegranate

AMERICA PLAYS BALL

Athletic field at Massanutten Academy, Woodstock VA, 1922.
Prints and Photographs Division, LC-USZ62-47329

BOX 808022 PETALUMA CA 94975

Pomegranate

AMERICA PLAYS BALL

Three boys watch the game in Huntingdon PA, July 1941.
Photograph by Edwin Rosskam
Prints and Photographs Division, LC-USF33-5211-M3

CA 94975

PETALUMA

BOX 808022

Pomegranate

AMERICA PLAYS BALL

US Coast Guard sailors play ball on shore-fast ice in a bay in the
Bering Sea, winter 1953.

Prints and Photographs Division, LC-DIG-ppmsca-06616

CA 94975

PETALUMA

BOX 808022

Pomegranate

117185

AMERICA PLAYS BALL

Men and women playing baseball in a park. Stereographic view, c. 1910.
Prints and Photographs Division, LC-USZ62-97854

CA 94975

PETALUMA

BOX 808022

Pomegranate

AMERICA PLAYS BALL

Japanese American batter from Farm Security Administration mobile
camp near Nyssa (OR) swings during a Sunday ball game, July 1942.

Photograph by Russell Lee

Prints and Photographs Division, LC-USF34-73586-D

CA 94975

PETALUMA

BOX 808022

Pomegranate

AMERICA PLAYS BALL

Choosing sides, Washington DC.
Prints and Photographs Division, LC-DIG-ppmsca-06613

CA 94975

PETALUMA

BOX 808022

Pomegranate

AMERICA PLAYS BALL

Farmers' baseball game near their mountain home in northern
Arkansas, August 1938.

Photograph by Dorothea Lange

Prints and Photographs Division, LC-USF34-018962-E

BOX 808022   PETALUMA   CA 94975

Pomegranate

AMERICA PLAYS BALL

Children's baseball game in front of a slag pile in Coaldale PA, August 1940.
Photograph by Jack Delano
Prints and Photographs Division, LC-USF34-41214-D

CA 94975

PETALUMA

BOX 808022

Pomegranate

AMERICA PLAYS BALL

Interracial team at Camp Lejeune, New River NC, March 1943.
Photograph by Roger Smith
Prints and Photographs Division, LC-USW3-22973-C

BOX 808022　PETALUMA　CA 94975

Pomegranate

AMERICA PLAYS BALL

Winding up for a pitch, Washington DC.
Prints and Photographs Division, LC-DIG-ppmsca-06617

AMERICA PLAYS BALL

Members of congressional baseball teams parade around the field
accompanied by an elephant, the Republican mascot, Washington DC,
May 3, 1926.

Prints and Photographs Division, LC-USZ62-94505

BOX 808022 PETALUMA CA 94975

Pomegranate

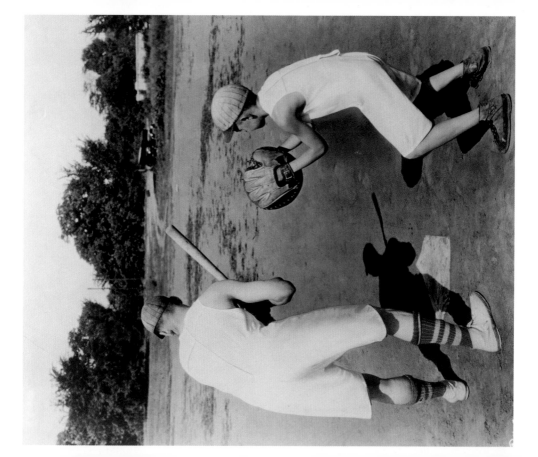

AMERICA PLAYS BALL

"Be unaware of your underwear," c. 1928.
Prints and Photographs Division, LC-USZ62-116211

BOX 808022   PETALUMA   CA 94975

Pomegranate

AMERICA PLAYS BALL

Baseball team at Eymard Seminary, Suffern NY.
Prints and Photographs Division, LC-USZ62-84359

BOX 808022   PETALUMA   CA 94975

Pomegranate

AMERICA PLAYS BALL

Baseball game between Japanese Americans at Manzanar
Relocation Camp, 1943.

Photograph by Ansel Adams

Prints and Photographs Division, LC-A351-3-M-6

BOX 808022   PETALUMA   CA 94975

Pomegranate

AMERICA PLAYS BALL

Farm Security Administration project baseball game in Shriever LA,
May 1940.

Photograph by Marion Post Wolcott

Prints and Photographs Division, LC-USF34-54345-D

BOX 808022   PETALUMA   CA 94975

Pomegranate

AMERICA PLAYS BALL

Virginia Smoot tagged out at third by Mabel Harvey during a junior
high school field day game, Washington DC, May 9, 1925.

Prints and Photographs Division, LC-USZ62-63995

CA 94975

PETALUMA

BOX 808022

Pomegranate

AMERICA PLAYS BALL

Senator George Pepper (R-PA, 1922–1927) and congressional pages
playing baseball in front of the US Capitol, March 25, 1924.

Prints and Photographs Division, LC-USZ-62-34138

CA 94975

PETALUMA

BOX 808022

Pomegranate

AMERICA PLAYS BALL

Boy swings and misses. Saturday morning game at Farm Security
Administration camp in Robstown TX, January 1942.

Photograph by Arthur Rothstein

Prints and Photographs Division, LC-USF34-24820-D

CA 94975

PETALUMA

BOX 808022

Pomegranate

AMERICA PLAYS BALL

Sunday ball game at Ellipse Park, Washington DC, between garage
workers and the employees' recreation association, July 1942.

Photograph by Marjory Collins

Prints and Photographs Division, LC-USF34-100542-E

BOX 808022   PETALUMA   CA 94975

Pomegranate

AMERICA PLAYS BALL

A uniformed soldier takes a swing.
Prints and Photographs Division, LC-DIG-ppmsca-06614

BOX 808022 PETALUMA CA 94975

Pomegranate

AMERICA PLAYS BALL

Students play baseball during recess in front of their one-room schoolhouse in Grundy County IA, October 1939.

Photograph by Arthur Rothstein

Prints and Photographs Division, LC-USF34-028420-D

CA 94975

PETALUMA

BOX 808022

Pomegranate

AMERICA PLAYS BALL

Team from Morris Brown College, Atlanta GA, c. 1900.
Prints and Photographs Division, LC-USZ62-114266

CA 94975

PETALUMA

BOX 808022

Pomegranate

AMERICA PLAYS BALL

Grade school game at recess, San Augustine TX, April 1939.
Photograph by Russell Lee
Prints and Photographs Division, LC-USF33-012140-M4

BOX 808022   PETALUMA   CA 94975

Pomegranate

AMERICA PLAYS BALL

Mothers-versus-daughters game at Shady Hill Country Day School, Chestnut Hill PA.

CA 94975

PETALUMA

BOX 808022

Pomegranate

AMERICA PLAYS BALL

Member of the "Dinkyrinks Nine" slides into home. Stereographic view, 1923.

Prints and Photographs Division, LC-DIG-ppmsca-06612

BOX 808022   PETALUMA   CA 94975

Pomegranate

AMERICA PLAYS BALL

Sandlot at Farm Security Administration Tulare camp for migrant
workers in Visalia CA, March 1940.

Photograph by Arthur Rothstein

Prints and Photographs Division, LC-USF34-24143-D

BOX 808022   PETALUMA   CA 94975

Pomegranate